A Commonplace Book

of Pentastichs

Other Books in Print by James Laughlin

JAMES LAUGHLIN

A Commonplace Book
of Pentastichs

EDITED WITH AN INTRODUCTION
BY HAYDEN CARRUTH

A NEW DIRECTIONS BOOK

Some of the poems in this volume were included in James Laughlin's *The Secret Room* (1997). "The Ancient Ocean" and "On Awakening" were first published in *DoubleTake*.

THANKS ARE MADE TO THE FOLLOWING FOR THEIR TEXTS OR TRANSLATIONS: *Walter Abish, Gilbert Adair, David Antin, Willis Barnestone, Jacques Barzun, Mary Beach, Bei Dao, Edwin Brock, William Bronk, Camilo José Cela, Margaret Jull Costa, Guy Davenport, Brendan Gill, David Hinton, Patricia Hougaard, Howard Isbell, Edgar Johnson, Donald Keene, Jane Kenyon, George Keyt, P. Lal, Lambros J. Lambros, J.B. Leishman, Jack Lindsay, Barry Magid, W.S. Merwin, Octavio Paz, Deborah Pease, Marjorie Perloff, Robert Pinsky, Edward Rice, Alastair Reid, Jerome Rothenberg, Charles Simic, Andrew Schelling, Frederick Smock, Gary Snyder, Antonio Tabucchi, Alan. S. Trueblood, Eleanor Trumbull, Anne Waldman, Eliot Weinberger, Barbara Wright, Bill Zavatsky.*

Manufactured in the United States of America
New Directions Book are published on acidfree paper.
First published clothbound by New Directions in 1998.
Published simultaneously in Canada by Penguin Books Canada Ltd.

Library of Congress Cataloging-in-Publication Data
Laughlin, James, 1914-
   A commonplace book of pentastichs / James Laughlin; edited
   with an introduction by Hayden Carruth.
      p.   cm.
ISBN 0-8112-1386-2 (clothbound: acid-free paper)
I. Carruth, Hayden, 1921–. II. Title.
   PS3523.A8245C66   1998
   811'.54—dc21   98–12968
                                               CIP

NEW DIRECTIONS BOOKS ARE PUBLISHED FOR JAMES LAUGHLIN
BY NEW DIRECTIONS PUBLISHING CORPORATION,
80 EIGHTH AVENUE, NEW YORK 10014

ᔈ Introduction

Commonplace books have been an engaging adjunct of literary performance for hundreds of years. Everyone knows this, and most of us, one way or another, have kept commonplace books of our own, notebooks in which we copy out fragments from our reading, anything that seems especially trenchant or felicitous. Often we add our own commentaries. Some such books are famous, of course, those assembled by William Byrd and Thomas Jefferson and W. H. Auden, for instance; but hundreds and hundreds have been published. Some scholars think the original commonplace books were kept by medieval philosophers and natural scientists for purposes of research and in preparing arguments; but this is fanciful. The idea is universal.

Who is surprised, consequently, to learn that James Laughlin, one of the most finely educated and widely acquainted editors and publishers of our time, has kept a commonplace book? He's a natural for it.

A more particular question is why has he cast his jottings into pentastichs, five-line verses. The reason must be deep in his unconscious memory. Probably he himself doesn't know. But Laughlin is a poet as well as an editor, a poet of acknowledged standing, and if we look at his poems of the past sixty years or so we find that he prefers, on one hand, a language of natural, nearly conversational plainness and, on the other, metrical forms that are arbitrary and artificial in the extreme. Not that he uses conventional rhyme and meter; he never does. But he likes to invent for himself tight prosodic restraints within which to arrange his phrasings. Isn't this the poetic impulse in general, or part of it? One way or another all poets do the same. At any rate it's hard to think of authentic exceptions. The pentastich is merely the most recent of Laughlin's inventions.

Of course you can find plenty of precedents. Five-line stanzas abound in any anthology. One thinks of Tennyson's "Tears, Idle Tears" or Poe's "To Helen," or perhaps Charles Olson's "fivers" in his *Maximus*. Or one remembers the *quintil* in French, the *lira* in Spanish. But for Laughlin the pentastich is not a stanza, it is a complete poem. Our commonest pentastich, in this sense, is undoubtedly the limerick, but five-line epigrams can be found from Empedocles to J. V. Cunningham. The Japanese *tanka*, a highly developed literary form, has influenced many Western poets, notably Adelaide Crapsey, whose "cinquains" in an unrhymed syllabic pattern of her own invention have a subtlety of movement that is wholly admirable. But to my mind these precedents have impinged on Laughlin's pentastichs scarcely at all. As the reader of this book (or any of his others) will find, Laughlin raids the classics, ancient and modern, with rapacious facility in search of what makes the substance of poetry, the substance of human thought and feeling, but in verbal usage he has not imitated anyone.

Laughlin has chosen his cited passages from an extraordinary range of sources, yet he himself is very much a presence among them. Some passages from foreign literatures he has translated himself, others he has taken from translations already existing, whichever is handiest; he has put them all into pentastichs and he hasn't refrained from excerpting or making necessary minor alterations, though I have seen the whole work in progress and I can verify that he has done no mischief. Then at the end he has placed a number of pentastichs derived from his own earlier poems—revisitings, so to speak. What a conglomeration! The wise, trivial, funny, poignant, even the foolish: a fine jumble. In effect it is an attestation to human existence in all its thoughtfulness and hunger, its fear and love and sexuality. For the reader it is a survey of literature that will never be found in a classroom—praise whatever gods may be—but indubitably will be found in loving and longstanding proximity on many a bedside table.

–HAYDEN CARRUTH

A Commonplace Book

of Pentastichs

A Great Emperor

Akbar, the greatest of the Mogul emperors, who
united the fiefdoms of India as far south as
the Godavari, was also a man of intellect. He
maintained at his court sages of all religions
and had the *Mahabharata* translated into Persian.

❧

An Exquisite Life

Robert Montesquiou, the exquisite model
for Proust's Charlus, kept bats in
silver cages, and for his famous receptions
had each room of his dwelling sprayed
with a different suggestive perfume.

❧

Trying to Please

Berenice cried when she couldn't fit her breast
into the Emperor's wine glass. She wanted to
have him think of her as a Grecian charmer. Her
brother, Agrippa, consoled her with the thought
we can't always make our bodies do what we want.

The God of the Sun and Fire

Glory to Agni, the high priest of the sacrifice.
We approach you, Agni, with reverential homage in
our thoughts, daily, both morning and evening.
You, the radiant, the protector of sacrifices,
the constant illuminator, be as a father to us.

Excerpt from the First Mandala of the Rig-Veda
(*c.* 1500 B.C.), abridged.

∾

The Applicant

First, are you our sort of person?
Do you wear a glass eye, false teeth
Or a crutch, a brace or a hook,
Rubber breasts or a rubber crotch,
Stitches to show something's missing?

Sylvia Plath, from *Ariel.*

∾

Enjoy the Passing Hour

There's no use asking, Leuconoe, what end the gods
have set for us, or consulting the Chaldean astrologers.
Better to enjoy what comes, whether Jove gives more
winters or this is the last. Cut short your hopes.
Reap the harvest of today, don't trust the morrow's.

Horace (abridged).

Two for One

The painter Schiele knew he was two people,
and that he needed separate women. When he
saw the Harms sisters in the street he hung
nude pictures of himself in his window. Edith
Harms married him. Adele became his model.

∾

The Talking Truck

In our town there's a young man who drives
a snappy red pickup. He has its sound
system wired so that when he passes you
on the road it will sing out a cheerful
"Have a good day." Greater love hath no truck.

∾

If I Die

What will you do, God, if Death takes me?
I am your jug (if someone breaks me?)
I am your drink (if curdling cakes me?)
I am your trim, your trade—it makes me
think: with me goes your meaning too.

Rainer Maria Rilke, *Possibility of Being.*
Trans. J. B. Leishman.

An Evening's Entertainment

For a Hollywood party in honor of Henry
Miller the hostess rented a starlet to keep
him amused. Things went well till the girl
rushed from the bedroom screaming: "All
the old bastard wants to do is bite my toes."

∾

Tripartite

My twin brother, Brendan, wears gloves that
Don't match. He says it's because he is
Two persons. He became three when he detached
His memory and sent it to live in Iowa. Too
Many things he doesn't want to think of again.

Brendan Gill.

∾

Logodaedaly

In the tradition of medieval logodaedalists,
Perec wrote a 284-page book with no "e's" in it,
like this: "It's all in vain, his subconscious
starts buzzing around in him again, buzzing around
and within him, choking and suffocating him."

George Perec, A Void. Trans. Gilbert Adair.

An Eskimo Song

I will walk with leg muscles which are
strong as the sinews of the shins of the
little caribou calf, strong as the shins
of the hare. I won't go towards the dark,
I'll walk only towards the light of day.

From the Anerca Collection.

∿

The Lovers

Radha looked on the god Krishna who desired only
her, who long had wanted dalliance with her. His face
was possessed with desire. It showed his passion
through tremblings of glancing eyes. It was like
a lotus pond with a pair of wagtails at play.

From the Sanskrit of Jayadeva's Gita-Govinda
(12th century). Trans. George Keyt.

∿

The Exiles

banished for their opinions to remote
parts of Russia are a little feared and by no
means confounded with ordinary mortals.
Dangerous people have that kind of attraction
which notorious Don Juans have for women.

Alexander Herzen, a passage from Childhood,
Youth and Exile. Trans. J. D. Duff.

I Travel Your Body

I travel your body, like the world,
your belly is a plaza full of sun,
your breasts two churches where blood
performs its own, parallel rites,
my glances cover you like ivy....

Octavio Paz, Sunstone (abridged). Trans. Eliot Weinberger.

∾

The Mime

Herondas was a mime who performed in wine
shops. I looked forward to his *Whorehouse
Manager,* but felt let down. It was about
a legal trial for rape. Nothing about a
brothel and Greek girls' hot tricks.

∾

An Existence of Exile

It was an existence of exile from the world.
He never saw a human face or figure, nor even
an animal; there were no familiar objects
along the way, there was no ground below, nor
sky above, yet the space was full of things.

Paul Bowles, from The Sheltering Sky.

Tempus Loquendi

To every thing there is a season, and a time to every
purpose under the heaven; a time to be born, and a
time to die ... a time to weep and a time to laugh ...
a time to mourn and a time to dance ... a time to
keep silence, and a time to speak....

From *Koheleth, the Book of Ecclesiastes* (abridged).

One Lost

When she saw how shamelessly I proclaimed
my lack of courage, she ceased to find me worthy
of pity. She considered me despicable. She left me
at once. It was too much. At the gate of the
hospital that evening she did not kiss me.

Louis-Fernand Céline, from *Journey to the
End of the Night*. Trans. H. P. Marks.

Time Is the Mercy of Eternity

What can you say in a poem?
Past forty, you've said it all....
The holiness of the real
is always there, accessible
in total immanence....

Kenneth Rexroth, from the *Collected Shorter Poems*.

The Emperor Makes a Poem

"And now the moon had set. The Emperor thought
of the girl's mother and wondered, making a poem
of the thought, with what feelings she had watched
the sinking of the autumn moon; 'for even the Men
Above the Clouds were weeping when it sank.'"

From Lady Murasaki's *The Tale of Genji*.
Trans. Arthur Waley.

❧

Time in India

The old man at the temple told me that Sita
was his grandmother. Sita, the wife of the
hero Rama, who cut off the nine heads of
Ravanna, the demon king of Ceylon. How long
ago was that? There is no time in India.

Cf. *The Ramayana*.

❧

The Afterlife

This afterlife from earlier
lives—it's not what we sighed
for! (Survival it may be.)
Tell me, mirror, what I know: "Oh,
your karma isn't what *you* decide."

M. L. Rosenthal, from *Offstage Music*.

Telling Tales

Herodotus was the "father of history," but now and then
a grain of salt is recommended. Sometimes he treated
hearsay as fact. For example, the Danube does not rise
in the Pyrenees and the sun's course is not affected
by wind. Plutarch wrote a treatise on his "malignity."

∽

Every Day Except Sunday:
A Triple Pentastich

the old ones visit the Supermarket.
It gives them something to do after
they've watched the soap operas on
TV, after they're dusted the house
and started something for dinner.

Very few of them have cars but the
Supermarket sends a bus around to
pick them up and take them home.
They haven't the money to buy much,
many of them live on relief, but

the bus is good advertising. The
clerks know most of them by their
first names. "How you doing today,
Margaret?" "Have a good day, Helen."
"You too, Joe." It's their antiphony.

Thy Treasure

The flatterer will quit thee in Adversity. But
the Fool will never forsake thee. If thou hid'st
thy Treasure upon Earth, how can'st thou expect
to find it in Heaven? Give not thy Tongue too
great a Liberty, lest it take thee Prizoner.

Edinburgh, 1713.

❧

The Revelation

There you will reveal
to me the things my soul desired,
and in a flash, O love,
there you will restore
what but a day ago you gave to me.

St. John of the Cross, *Spiritual Canticle*.
Trans. Willis Barnstone.

❧

Arli

She had a dog named Arli whom she had
taught to think and typewrite on a special
machine with huge keys that Arli could press
with his nose. Arli's messages were right on,
you could ask him questions about the dead.

The Fantasist

Ronald Firbank the decadent novelist liked
to play out his fantasies. When Lady Cunard
invited him to lunch at the London Ritz he
studied the menu with care and ordered *one*
pea, which he sent back because it was cold.

⌒

An Unusual Girl

In Lucerne beautiful Birgita liked to circle
the Matterhorn in her Piper Cub. Evenings you
might find her with her friends in her bathtub
enjoying live fish in an intimate way while
the phonograph played Schubert's *Trout Quintet.*

⌒

The Affirmation

Sophia Antonova wished me good-bye
as if she had not heard a word of my
impious hope, but she turned for an instant
and declared in a firm voice—
"Peter Ivanovich is an inspired man."

Joseph Conrad, concluding passage from
Under Western Eyes.

Fair Women

Fair women I saw passing where she passed;
and none among them women, to my vision;
but were like nothing save her shadow cast.
I praise her in no cause save verity's,
none other dispraise, if ye comprehend me.

Guido Cavalcanti (1255-1300), trans. Ezra Pound.

∾

A Ceremony

If he has to micturate at night, Bill likes
to go outside into the darkness to do it.
As he pees he looks up at the stars and
listens for the hooting of owls. He says it
makes him feel truly a part of nature.

∾

I Feel Drunk All the Time

Jesus it's beautiful! Great
mother of big apples, it's a
pretty world. You're a bastard Mr. Death
and I wish you didn't have
no look-in here.

Kenneth Patchen, Collected Poems.

A Visit to Harlem

When I was young we'd go up to Harlem to the
Lynx, where if you put a five dollar bill on
the edge of the table, a lovely young girl
would daintily lift her skirt and pick it
up with her snatch without using her hands.

✑

Difficulty in Henry James

Henry James had from the middle of his writing
life to its end an increasing reputation for
being difficult beyond reason: obscure in style,
tenuous in theme, and subtle to the point of
exasperation in both detail and point of view.

R. P. Blackmur, from *Studies in Henry James*,
ed. Veronica Makowsky.

✑

This Foreign Language

You come into the world not speaking it.... It's
their language and they've spoken it...
and you haven't spoken anything... you've been
involved in looking and feeling.... And they keep
speaking their own foreign language.

David Antin, from "Real Estate" in the book *Tuning*.

The First Time

It was the first time we had made love.
I asked her what she would like me to do
to give her pleasure. But she wouldn't
tell me. She said I must find out for
myself. It would be better so.

∾

The Viper

For years I was under the spell of that woman.
She used to appear in my office completely naked
and perform contortions that defy imagination,
simply to draw my poor soul into her orbit
and above all to wring from me my last penny.

Nicanor Parra, *Antipoems*. Trans. W. S. Merwin.

∾

Vienna

"Vienna," said the doctor, "the bed into
which the common people climb, docile
with toil, and out of which the nobility
fling themselves ferocious with dignity,
I can still remember all of it today."

Djuna Barnes, from *Nightwood*.

The Double Heads

Upon one body
Double heads opposing chop-
Stick beaks in order,
Peck peck pecking off to death,
One bird: both heads and body.

Japanese linked verse, *c.* 1500. Author
unknown. Trans. Edwin Brock.

∾

The Fulfillment

No man can utterly fulfill
what's in his heart but when he does
it seems but a little thing. When
he is satisfied his love is perfect
his heart proves the defect.

Aimeric de Belenoi (1217-42). Trans. from
Langue d'Oc, Paul Blackburn.

∾

Fidelio: Ezra Pound

Ezra and Olga and I were staying at the Goldene Rose
in Salzburg. We went to hear Toscanini conducting
Fidelio in the Festspielhaus. Ezra never liked Beethoven.
After ten minutes he rose up and shouted: "What can you
expect, the man had syphillis?" Toscanini didn't miss a beat.

The French

The French are such an orderly race.
They tell how the grande horizontale
Liane de Pougy offered her lovers
only the upper part of her body, the
lower being reserved for her husband.

∾

The Visit of Eros

Philodemus remembers how we first made the bedlamp
tipsy with oil, then let it go out. We knew there
are times when Eros wants no witness. We had the
bed, the lovers' friend, to teach us Aphrodite's
secrets, the things of which we seldom dare to speak.

∾

Hard Times

The unquiet and feverish state of mind in which
Dickens finished *Hard Times* was more than the aftermath
of intense effort.... Significant was the mingling
of his feelings about his private life with his realization
of how much was wrong with England and the world.

Edgar Johnson, from Charles Dickens:
His Tragedy and Triumph (abridged).

The Bharata

As the body cherishes the food it eats, as
an ambitious servant seeking promotion
serves willingly a master of noble birth,
so all poets serve and cherish Bharata,
as it was in the making of this magnificent epic.

> *Bharata:* a prince descended from the Pandavas, rivals
> of the Kauravas; from the *Mahabharata.* Trans. P. Lal.

∾

Flaubert's Handbook of Clichés

Extirpate: Verb only applied to hearsay and corns.
Free Trade: Cause of all business troubles.
Frog: Female of the toad.
Gaming: Wax indignant at this fatal passion.
Genius: No point admiring… it's a neurosis.

> From *The Dictionary of Accepted Ideas.*
> Trans. Jacques Barzun.

∾

Vedanta

The primary elements of Vedanta are Vidya, the
absolute, and Maya, the illusory. In Vedanta
there is no evil as such, only the unreal
appearance of evil or ignorance such as a barren
woman, a horned hare, or water in a mirage.

The Canticle of the Creatures

Be praised, O Lord, for Sister Moon and
the stars; Thou hast formed them in the
heavens, clear, precious and beautiful.
Be praised, O Lord, for Sister Water, the
which is so useful, humble and precious.

St. Francis of Assisi, fragment.
Trans. Eleanor L. Turnbull.

ᔉ

A Health Problem

I saw on TV that millions of men suffer from
toenail fungus. That's awful, but my sickness
is worse. I suffer from corrosion of the soul.
I no longer go to church and I read subversive
books about Krishna and Buddha. No pill for that.

ᔉ

Paolo and Francesca

We read of Lancelot, by love constrained:
Alone, suspecting nothing, at our leisure.
Sometimes at what we read our glances joined,
Looking from the book each to the other's eyes.
And then the color in our faces drained....

Dante, Inferno, fifth canto. Trans. Robert Pinsky.

Freedom from Rebirth

He whose mind is unsteady and whose heart
is impure, never reacheth the goal, but is born
again and again. But he whose mind is steady
and whose heart is pure, reacheth the goal,
and having reached it is born no more.

From the *Katha Upanishad* (*c.* 900 B.C.).
Trans. Swami Prabhavanada.

❧

Vigils

It is repose in light, neither fever nor languor, on
a bed or on a meadow.... It is the friend neither violent
nor weak.... It is the beloved neither tormenting nor
tormented.... Air and the world not sought. Life....
Was it really this? And the dream grew cold.

Artur Rimbaud, from *The Illuminations*. Trans. Louise Varèse.

❧

A Woman of the Sankhini Type

She is of medium build, her foot is long and covered
with prominent blood vessels. She has a yoni which
is ever moist with love fluid that has the smell
of salt. Her temper is violent in spasm when she
thrusts her nails into the flesh of her partner.

From the Sanskrit *Kokkokam*.

The Immeasurable Boundaries

Heraclitus wrote that we would not discover
the boundaries of the soul even if we traveled
all the world's roads. At eighty I've traversed
a good many of them, but now I've stopped walking.
The boundaries of the soul are immeasurable.

∾

Good Philosophy

When I give you an apple, if you love me
from your heart, exchange it for your
maidenhead. But if your feelings are what
I hope they are not, please take the apple
and reflect on how short-lived is beauty.

Plato.

∾

A Wintry Christmas

It's winter, so cold, and three feet of
snow. I think of Villon's lines about
the hungry wolves. "Sur le Noël, morte
saison, lorsque les loups vivent de vent."
Wolves have nothing to eat but the wind.

Inscriptio Fontis

Stay here thy way, O voyager,
   for terrible now is the heat;
Thy tired feet can go no farther now,
Balm here for weariness is in
   sweet reclining.

Andrea Navagero. (16th-century Latin).
Trans. Ezra Pound.

∾

God in Politics

"You may believe you're descended from monkeys.
I don't believe it. I think you're a creature
of God. I believe that God created heaven and
earth. I think you have a right to insist that
Godless evolution not be taught to your children."

Patrick J. Buchanan. Excerpt from a campaign speech.

∾

The Way of Renunciation

A selfless man who has renounced
the fruit of his action attains peace.
But the man who is not selfless
and who is led by desire is attached
to the fruit and therefore is bound.

From the Bhagavad Gita. Trans. Swami Nikhilananda.

Kankha-Revata

A campfire at midnight
eats at the circle of darkness
subduing the shadows
for all who pass.
Ever so are the Tathagata's words.

> Tathagata: one who incarnates enlightenment.
> Written in Pali script on palm leaves (*c.* 90 B.C.).
> Trans. Andrew Schelling and Anne Waldman.

❧

The Hetaera

Ani Laesca, a Greek cocotte who worked Zurich,
could have modeled for Apelles. I never fingered
her expensive flesh, but when she wasn't engaged
she liked to play pool in the Dolder, regaling
me with the kinks of the richest men in Europe.

❧

The Writer at Work

On opening night of his play *Under Milk Wood,*
Dylan Thomas is backstage lying on his tummy,
writing new lines for the cast: "Organ Morgan
at his bedroom window playing chords on the
sill for the fishwife gulls in Donkey Street."

The Hair Shirt

Eleanor of Aquitaine, a spirited girl who
wrote troubadour cansos, married at fifteen
the king who slept in a hair shirt and became
Saint Louis. "I thought I had married a
man, but found I had married a monk."

∾

The Courtship of Thomas More's Daughters:
A Double Pentastich

In his *Utopia* Thomas More prescribed that couples
should see each other stark-naked before marriage.
When Sir William Roper askt for the hand of a More
daughter he was led to a chamber where both girls were
abed. More whippt the sheete off, exposing the modest

maidens on their backs, with their smocks raised to the arme-
pitts. But at once they turned on their bellies.
Quoth Roper: "I have seen both sides," and he slappt
one daughter on the buttock. "Thou art mine," he ex-
claimed. And in this was all the trouble of the wooeing.

Adapted from Aubrey's *Brief Lives.*

What's New?

Last year the Serbs took 200 Muslims out into
the woods and shot them. What's new? A thousand
years ago when the Indian Muslims overran Java
they lopped off the heads of a hundred Buddhist
monks who were praying at the temple of Borobudur.

∿

The Linguist

The poet Edouard Roditi mastered a dozen
languages. He got high-paying jobs for
simultaneous translations at international
conferences. His pride was a Portuguese-
Turkish performance, done without a slip.

∿

A Happy Ending

After a difficult life with many
disappointments the poet Larus,
at ninety, drifted away into
the land of Otherwhere. He couldn't
remember anything, even who he was.

The Joy of Your Charm

The charm of how you are gives me such joy
that my desire pleasures me every day.
Now totally and in full you mistress me,
how overmastered I am, I can scarce say.
Before I saw you I determined to love you.

Guilhem Cabestanh (1190-1212).
Trans. Paul Blackburn.

∾

Hunger

The hunger of the rich man
knows no end,
the man & the woman, both insatiable,
reduce the world's flesh to a sauce
& smear it over their wrists and thighs....

Jerome Rothenberg, from *New Selected Poems*.

∾

His Hand: Two Lines from Lear, Act V

Now that he's old and foolish,
his hand smells of mortality.
Wash it as he may, he can't regain
the scent of the time when lovely
hands longed to touch and caress it.

The Wrong Button

Fine people. Aristocrats running the family business.
I was so honored when they put me on their board.
Then disaster. A careless girl pushed the wrong
computer button. All the sales records erased.
Everything gone. The end of a great company.

∾

Singing Her Name

There where this lady's loveliness appeareth
is heard a voice which goes before her ways
and seems to sing her name with such sweet praise
that my mouth fears to speak what name she heareth,
and my heart trembles for the grace she weareth.

Guido Cavalcanti (1255-1300). Trans. Ezra Pound.

∾

The Wise Man

Crusty Diogenes was homeless, he lived in
a tub with stray dogs. But his wit ruled
Athens. He pointed out that philosophy can
often turn a young man from the love of a
beautiful body to love for a beautiful mind.

A Trip Through Africa

Ages ago an archeologist, Albert, alias Arthur,
ably attended an archaic African armchair
affair at Antibes, attracting attention as an
archeologist and atheist.... Albert advocated
assisting African ants. All are astounded.

> Walter Abish, from *Alphabetical Africa*, a novel in which
> each chapter contains only words beginning with the successive
> letters of the alphabet. The form originated in the Middle Ages.

∾

The Happy Poets

It's my delight to recite
my poems in the arms of
an intelligent girl and
to please her dear ear
with what I've written.

> Propertius, 11, XIII.

∾

Wanderer's Night-Song

You who look down from the heavens to comfort
our pain and sorrows and my doubly wretched
heart, bring me refreshment, I'm weary with
the struggle—why this rapture and unrest?
Let your peace descend upon me and remain.

> Adapted from Goethe.

Of Zeno the Philosopher

Neither winter's cold, nor endless rain,
Nor blazing sun can overpower him.
Terrible illness does not move him.
Night and day, unbending, he pursues
His discipline to the utmost.

Diogenes Laertius, Lives and Opinions of Eminent Philosophers
(c. 200-250 A.D.). Trans. Barry Magid.

The Seashell

Someone brought me a seashell.
Singing inside is a sea from a map.
My heart fills up with water
and a little tiny fish, silvery, shadowy.
Someone brought me a seashell.

Garcia Lorca. Trans. Alan S. Trueblood.

The Secret Line in Loving

There is a sacred, secret line in loving
which attraction and even passion cannot cross—
even if lips draw near in awful silence
and love tears at the heart.
Friendship is weak and useless here....

Anna Akhmatova. Trans. Jane Kenyon.

The Young Priest

She had a friend, a young priest,
who would sit by her bed for
hours, just watching her nude
body. He never spoke or touched
her. A new form of prayer?

∾

Language

I resist philosophy, systems.
But I've always admired Unamuno,
whose name means
"one world"
but in no known language.

Frederick Smock.

∾

The Honeybee

You do everything, Melissa, just the way
your namesake the honeybee does.
When you're kissing me honey drips
from your lips, but when you ask
for money you have a sharp sting.

Marcus Argentarius (fl. 1st century A.D.).

The Young Deer

The under leaves of the lespedeza
When dew is gathering
Must be cold:
On the autumn moor
The young deer are crying.

Lady Sagami (10th-century Japan). Trans. Arthur Waley.

∾

Want

I do not want to be a
Mammologist
I would like a lot
Of rupees and go and
Use them in a store

Anne Waldman.

∾

Flaubert's Earlier Lives

My present self is the consequence of all my vanished
selves. I was boatman on the Nile … a procurer in
Rome … I died during the Crusades from eating
too many grapes on the beach in Syria … I was pirate
and monk … perhaps Emperor of the East, who knows?

From a letter to George Sand, 29 September
1866. Trans. Francis Steegmuller.

Women

There is no fury like a woman searching
for a new lover. When we see a woman meekly
chewing the cud beside her second husband,
it is hard to imagine how brutally, pettily
and implacably she has got rid of the first.

Cyril Connolly, The Unquiet Grave.

∾

On Wealth

What may be achieved by a man who has gained
great wealth is like watching a fight between
elephants having climbed to the top of a hill.
Let riches be gathered; it is the steel that cuts
through the pride of foes; nothing is sharper.

From the medieval Tamil of Tiruvalluver's
Tirukkural. Trans. A.N.K. Aiyangar.

∾

The Healer

Hippocrates of Cos, the great physician,
left us the message that health is the
greatest of all possible human blessings,
and that we should learn how by our own
thought to derive benefit from illnesses.

In the Auvergne

A shepherdess is waiting for her lover by
a big oak. But he doesn't come. "Have I
been deserted? I thought he loved me, and
I love him so much." The evening star
rises; she is still alone, and weeping.

A folksong.

◦

Her Beauty

Criseyde was this lady's name aright;
As to my dame, in al Troyes citee
Nas noon so fair, for passing every wight
So aungellyk was hir natyf beautee
That lyk a thing immortal semed she....

Chaucer, from Troilus and Criseyde.

◦

Voltaire and Christianity

Voltaire's *Republican Ideas* called the Christian
priesthood an outrage against the Gospels.
The *Catechism of the Normal Man* made plain
that "Detest your enemy like yourself" was
the great maxim of Christianity.

Wayne Andrews, from Voltaire.

On Awakening

When you awake, say to yourself—Today
I shall encounter meddling, ingratitude,
violence, cunning, jealousy, self-seeking,
all of them the results of men not
knowing what is good and what's evil.

Marcus Aurelius Antoninus , from *To Himself.*

∾

Swearing

Do not swear by the heavens, because
they are the throne of God. Do not
swear by the earth, as it is his
footstool. Do not swear at all; let your
yes be your yes, and your no your no.

From the *Logia of Yeshua.* Trans. Guy Davenport.

∾

Human Society

I experienced sometimes that the most
sweet and tender, the most innocent and
encouraging society may be found in any
natural object, even for the poor misanthrope
and most melancholy man.

Thoreau, from *Walden.*

The Truth

Truth and right are my bases.
I hate frauds and hypocrites.
And if I vacillate sufficiently
avoiding them
my rancor sinks, and I find all is well.

Peire Cardenal (1225-72). Trans. Paul Blackburn.

༄

After Death

The First Bardo. From the moment of death
and for sometimes four days afterwards,
the Knower, in the case of the person deceased,
is in a very deep sleep or trance, unaware
that it has been separated from the human body.

The Tibetan Book of the Dead, trans. W. Y. Evans-Wentz.
Bardo: state between death and rebirth.

༄

The Good Life

Dr. Pangloss told Candide: "All events are linked
together in the best of worlds; if you had not been
driven out of a castle by hard kicks upon your hinder
parts for daring to make love to Cunegund, you
would not be here now eating citrons and pistachio nuts."

Voltaire, the conclusion of *Candide* (abridged).

After the Flood

As soon as the idea of the flood had abated,
a hare paused in the clover and bell-flowers
and prayed to the rainbow through the spider's
web. What jewels gleamed in hiding....
What flowers gazed all about them.

Arthur Rimbaud, from the *Illuminations*.
Trans. Helen Rootham.

∾

The Good Life

Nabokov remembers that when he was young,
early in July his grandfather's carriage
and a team of horses would be loaded on a
railroad flatcar for the trip across Europe
to Biarritz in France for the annual holiday.

∾

The Two Goddesses: Demeter and Persephone

Nothing about the Eleusinian Mysteries
was so striking as the initiates' awe
of Demeter's gift, the grain and their hope
of life after death. The ear of grain
is the most perfect epoptic mystery.

Carl Kerenyi, from *Eleusis*. Trans. Ralph Manheim.

Stories

The Seller of Stories lowered his arm and
held out a hand to me as if he were offering
me something. I give you tonight's moon, he
said, and I give you whatever story you feel
like hearing. I know you want to hear a story.

Antonio Tabucchi, from *Requiem*.
Trans. Margaret Jull Costa.

∿

The Ancient Ocean

Ancient ocean, crystal-waved, you resemble those
bluish marks on the battered backs of cabin boys;
you are a vast bruise inflicted upon the body
of earth; I love this comparison. You recall
the crude origin of man. I salute you, ocean!

From Lautréamont's *Maldoror*. Trans. Guy Wernham.

∿

The Idols of Japan

In the island of Zipangu their idols are fashioned
in a variety of shapes, some having the heads
of oxen, some of swine, of dogs, and other
animals.... The ceremonies practiced before their
gods are too wicked and diabolical to be related.

From *The Travels of Marco Polo*. Trans. Manuel Komroff.

In Hac Spe Vivo

The apogee in the career of the great
philosopher Wittgenstein was when he
phoned Bertie Russell to tell him he
had discovered a cure for the common
cold. But no, alas, he hadn't found it.

"In this hope I live," motto on Pericles' shield,
Shakespeare's play, Act II, Scene II.

≈

The Anglo-Saxon Chronicle

This year long dragons swam in fire
across the sky in Northumbria.
This was the year of the great gale.
And this year died Harthacanute:
Everything he did was unworthy of a king.

Adapted by Guy Davenport.

≈

In Hiding

The room seems to be empty. Covers heaped
on the bed, pillows on the floor. Where
can you be? Then mewing, like a cat's, comes
from under the bed. I pull you out by a
leg. Please don't play this game again.

The Russian Girl

The little Russian girl who kept Tenn cheerful
when he was rehearsing a play, usually got her
way, as when I picked her up at the Ritz to
go to dinner and she asked the concierge which
was the most expensive restaurant in the area.

∽

Epiphany, Anne Carson

Holding the gifts on their knees they rode carefully
over the steppes and tableland and across long
frozen afternoons dusted with diamonds.
Nothing so precious had ever been known.
Treasure bursts at the tip of the heart.

∽

The Story of Happiness

Happiness, unknown woman,
There's a childhood picture
Of the two of us,
Your hands are covering my eyes,
All but your arms are cut off.

Charles Simic, from *Walking the Black Cat.*

Betrothal in Assam

Among the Nagas of Assam unmarried girls sleep
in the granary door where bachelors wearing cowry
shells as medals of prowess come to visit them.
When a girl gets pregnant they line up the men
and she can choose the one she'd like to marry.

District Commissioner Mills, anecdotal.

∾

The Invitation to Make Love

Show her drawings of animals making love, then
of humans. The sight of erotic creatures such
as geese will make her curious. Write amorous
messages to her on palm leaves. Tell her your
dreams about her. Tickle her toes with your finger.

From the Sanskrit, Vatsyayana's Kama Sutra.
Trans. Alain Daniélou.

∾

Procurement

They met at M.I.T. Her family was Swiss.
They were in arms procurement. They had a
villa on the lake near Geneva. A brawny girl.
She took his virginity as if she were picking
an edelweiss. But he was given a job in the firm.

The Beloved Clown

The well-born but impoverished Boston poet
Jack Wheelwright was beloved in society for
his eccentricities. One night, on entering
a ballroom, he got under a rug and crawled
the length of it to offer a lily to the hostess.

❧

The Merry Life

I return to my cask. Up, lads, and to the
wine! Gulp it down, mes enfants, in brimming
cups. Of if you don't like it, leave it alone....
I'm not one of those tiresome Germans who
make their comrades drink by brute force.

François Rabelais, from *Gargantua and Pantagruel.*
Trans. J. M. Cohen.

❧

The Great Mother

Not all those who pass
In front of the Great Mother's chair
Get past with only a stare.
Some she looks at their hands
To see what sort of savages they were.

Gary Snyder.

The Blindfolded Lovers

In Magritte's painting, *Les Amants,* the lovers
have cloths over their heads while they're
kissing. That can't be much fun. But maybe
the fun is for each to kiss an ideal lover they've
never encountered and are only imagining.

❧

The Born Poet

Stesichoros of Sicily had no choice
but to become a poet. One day as
he lay in his cradle a nightingale
flew down and lit on his lips. The
little baby began to sing at once.

❧

The King-Swan

In a great lake there lived a king-swan named
Passion. He spent his days in pastimes. One day
death visited him in the form of an owl. "Where do
you come from?" asked the swan. "I came because
I heard of your great virtues," replied the owl.

From the *Panchatantra* (Kashmir, 200 B.C.).
Trans. A.W. Ryder.

Of Knowledge

We should make the knowledge of others our
own. Too often we resemble the man who
needing fire goes to his neighbor's to get it
but having found it he stays to warm
himself, forgetting his family at home.

> Michel de Montaigne. Trans. George B. Ives.

∾

The Lover's Complaint

I swear I do not ask too much of heaven:
O make that thoughtless girl
Who yesterday made me
Her spoils of war either love me
Or let me share her bed to prove I love her.

> Ovid, from the *Ars Amatoria.* Trans. Horace Gregory.

∾

The Conqueror

Alexander the Great was a severe disciplinarian.
If on the march to India a soldier broke the rules
he would be bound and small stones would
be stuffed down his throat till he suffocated.
It's odd that no one can find Alexander's tomb.

A Lullaby

Golden slumbers kiss your eyes,
Smiles awake you when you rise,
Sleep, pretty wantons, do not cry,
And I will sing a lullaby:
Rock them, rock them, lullaby.

Thomas Dekker. First stanza.

∾

Ladies Fighting

In Yorkshire late happen'd a desperate fight
'Tween a *Jacobite* lady and a *Williamite*,
'Twas fought with such courage no man could do more,
Nor the like was ne're known 'tween two women before;
For each met in the field with her sword by her side....

The Pepys Ballads (1690), ed. Hyder Rollings (abridged).

∾

The Crane

Go away, crane! Leave the garden!
You have not told my love,
the prince of the seashore,
the torment that I suffer.
Go away, crane! Leave the garden!

From the Tamil *Shilappadikaram* (300 A.D.). Trans. Alain Daniélou.

The Locust

Locust, beguiler of my loves and persuader of sleep,
mimic of nature's lyre, play for me a tune with your
talking wings to deliver me from the pains of care
and of love. In the morning I'll give you a fresh
green leek and drops of dew sprayed from my mouth.

Meleager of Gadara (fl. 60 B.C.).

⤳

In Vino Veritas

As he excelled in that licentious merriment which
wine incites, Rochester's friends encouraged him
in excess and he willingly indulged it. He was
for five years together continually drunk, so much
inflamed as not to be master of himself.

The Life and Death of John, Earl of Rochester,
Bishop Gilbert Burnet, D.D.

⤳

The Career Girl

Theodora was the greatest empress of Byzantium,
the daughter of a bearkeeper at the Constantinople
zoo. She was so good a courtesan that she was
married by the Emperor Justinian. He made her
joint ruler, but she was smarter and was the boss.

Lambros J. Lambros, anecdotal.

The Living Branch

If I existed as a tree
I would not be a conifer, cone-bearing.
My nature would be deciduous, a long
Process of leaves falling, falling
From the living branch.

Deborah Pease, The Feathered Wind.

∾

Lo Khor (Year Wheel)

In the center is a magic square; the numbers add
up to 15 in any direction.

492
357
816

The numbers
in the square are used to determine the most
appropriate day to undertake a project.

From the Tibetan Astrological Calendar.

∾

Lines

In the *Dhammapada* it is written
that the body is a strong fortress
made up of bones plastered with
flesh and blood, wherein lurk
pride, deceit, decay and death.

The Long Feet People

Pliny relates in his *Natural History* that
in Iluria there's a race with feet a *pes*
long, turned backwards, with 16 toes. On
hot days they lie on their backs, using
their feet to shade themselves from heat.

∿

Tout en Ordre

At Versailles only the Queen may have pompons
on her coach-covers; fastened with nails, and of
any color she pleases. Duchesses have
blue covers. Wives of eldest sons of dukes
have red covers. Widows have black velvet.

> From *Historical Memoirs*, Le Duc de Saint-Simon
> (1788). Trans. Lucy Morton.

∿

La Poésie

At my Swiss school Maître Jacquet was fierce when
he was coaching hockey but tender teaching us
French poetry. I could recite reams of Sully
Prudhomme: "Des yeux sans nombre ont vu l'aurore;
maintenant ils dorment au fond des tombeaux."

Cabestan

"It is Cabestan's heart in the dish.
No other taste shall change this."

The betrayed husband has killed
the lady's lover and served up his
heart for dinner. When she realizes
the monstrosity she throws herself
from the window of the castle.

See Ezra Pound, *Canto IV*.

∾

Wittgenstein's Ladder

My propositions are elucidatory in this way:
he who understands me finally recognizes
them as senseless, when he has climbed out
through them, on them, over them. (He must
throw away the ladder after climbing it.)

From the *Tractatus*. Ed. Marjorie Perloff.

∾

Who I Am

I hereby declare myself world-wide, oviparous,
giraffe, haggard sinophobic, and hemi-
spherical. I quench my thirst in the
wellsprings of the atmosphere that laughs
concentrically and farts with my uncertainty.

Max Jacob from "The Cock and the Pearl,"
Le Cornet à Dés. Trans. Bill Zavatsky.

Le Temps Perdu

All that elegant refinement of sensibility,
but when Proust's beloved mother died
he gave her furniture to a male brothel,
and the scholars have discovered that Albertine
was a handsome but uneducated taxi driver.

❧

Contentment

Père Ubu: by my green candle, shitter, certainly
I'm content. I'm a captain of dragoons, I'm King
Wenceslas' confidential officer. I've been decorated
with the Order of the Red Eagle of Poland. I'm
ex-King of Aragon, what more do you want?

Alfred Jarry, *Ubu Roi.* Trans. Barbara Wright.

❧

A Lover's Oath

Khiron swore to Ionis that no one, woman or
man, would ever be dearer to him. But we
know lovers' oaths don't penetrate to
celestial ears. Now he's mad for a pretty
boy, and poor Ionis has a broken heart.

Callimachus of Cyrene, b. 310 B.C.

Joyce's Words

Joyce maims words. Why? Because meanings
have been dulled, then lost, then perverted
by their connotations, until their effect on
the mind is no longer what it was when they
were fresh, but grows rotten as *poi.*

William Carlos Williams, from a symposium
on Joyce and *Finnegans Wake.*

∾

The Long Sleep

Let us live, Lesbia, and let us love,
caring nothing what people say about us.
Suns set and rise again, but when our sun
sets, that brief light, there will be
only a night of perpetual slumber.

Catullus V (abridged).

∾

Life Story

After you've been to bed together for the first time,
without the advantage of any prior acquaintance,
the other party very often says to you,
Tell me about yourself, I want to know all about you,
what's your story? And maybe they really do....

Tennessee Williams (abridged).

The Conversation:
A Double Pentastich

It always begins about three hours after
dark when most humans are asleep. Then
the barking of the four dogs on the farms
nearby commences. The voice of each dog
is readily distinguishable by its tone.

They never all speak at once. One will
begin and the others answer in turn. It's
a kind of music and it's a conversation.
But what do they talk about, what are
they telling each other? I wish I knew.

❧

The Labyrinth of Lines

As the years pass, he fills the empty
space with images of mountains, islands,
houses and people. Just before he dies,
he discovers that the patient labyrinth
of lines traces the image of his own face.

Jorge Luis Borges, *The Creator*. Trans. Alastair Reid.

The Goddess of Torment

To thee clepe I, thou goddesse of torment,
Thou cruel Furie, sorwing ever in peyne;
Help me, that am the sorwful instrument
That helpeth lovers, as I can, to pleyne,
For wel sit it, the sothe for to seyne....

Chaucer, Troilus and Criseyde.

❧

The Cadence of the World

I noticed a lightness that moved me. It probably
was how things were, myself included, all of us
transparent in the cadence of the world. A coming
and going, urging and denying, and in between,
untouchable, the way of existence.

Gottfried Benn, Primal Vision.
Trans. E. B. Ashton.

❧

The Life of Chivalry

So then it was that she and Sir Gawaine
went out of the castle and supped in a
pavilion, and there was made a bed and
Sir Gawaine and Lady Ettard went
there to bed together for two nights.

Sir Thomas Malory, from Le Morte d'Arthur.

The Growth of Love

I see Love grow resplendent in her eyes
with such great power and such noble thought
as hold therein all gracious ecstasies,
from them there moves a soul so subtly wrought
that all compared thereto are set at naught.

Guido Cavalcanti, trans. Ezra Pound.

∾

Easter Monday

An enormous chocolate egg surrounds the day,
Its pieces cheap and gritty to the teeth; we look out
Through cellophane, company with the yellow cotton
                                        chicks.
Outside it rains; we see the splashes covering the sky,
Hear it swish on an Indian file of motor cars which climbs
                                        the hill.

Edwin Brock, from Invisibility Is the Art of Survival (1972).

∾

A Classic Question

"Ingenium nobis ipsa puella facit."
Propertius wrote that it's the girl
who makes the poems. But is the obverse
true? Will poems make a girl? I'm
really not so certain about that.

The Manyoshu

She wrote to the poet that she
loved the embrace of his words.
He stopped adoring the moon
and covered many pages with
more of them for her pleasure.

> *The Manyoshu* (760 A.D.) is the classic
> collection of early Japanese verse.

⌒

Dinner with Trimalchio

The course that followed was spaced around a circular tray
where over the twelve signs of the Zodiac the chef had put
the most appropriate food: a pair of testicles and kidneys
over Gemini...virgin sowbelly on Virgo...over Scorpio
a crawfish...a lobster on Capricorn...on Aquarius a goose....

> From *The Satyricon of Petronius Arbiter*,
> trans. William Arrowsmith.

⌒

Cleomenes on Death

Doest thou thinke it a glorie for thee
to seek death, which is the easiest
matter, and the presentest unto any man;
and yet, wretche that thou art, thou fliest it
more cowardly & shamefully than battell.

> Plutarch, chapter on Agis and Cleomenes in the *Lives of*
> *Noble Grecians and Romans*. Trans. Sir Thomas North.

At the Sky's Edge

Love among the mountains: eternity that patience
of the earth simplifies our human sounds: one
arctic-thin cry from deep antiquity until now:
rest, weary traveler, a wounded ear's already
laid your dignity bare, one arctic-thin cry.

Bei Dao. Trans. David Hinton.

∾

De Corpore Hominum

When Pound translated De Gourmont's
Psysique de l'Amour did he really
believe the Frenchman's theory that sperm
rising to the brain produces creativity
or did he just assume it was a joke?

∾

Mortality

Preparing to die, the French poet Alain
Bosquet wrote: "No more me tomorrow;
my lines will be flabby as a fried egg
and void of meaning; no more me tomorrow;
the world won't even notice my absence."

Desires and Death

A man acteth according to the desires to which
he clingeth. After death he goeth to the next
world bearing in his mind the subtle impressions
of his deeds; and after reaping the harvest of
his deeds, he returneth to the world of action.

From the Brihadaranyaka Upanishad.
Trans. W.Y. Evans-Wentz.

❧

The Man of Tao

The non-action of the wise man is not inaction.
It is not studied. It is not shaken by anything.
The sage is quiet because he is not moved,
Not because he wills to be quiet.
Still water is like glass.

Fragment from Thomas Merton's version of
The Way of Chuang Tzu (1965).

❧

Desiderius Erasmus

His name was Gerard Gerard, which he translated into
Desiderius Erasmus: he loved not Fish, though borne
in a Fish-towne. He was begot (as they say) behind
dores. He was a tender Chitt, and his mother would not
entrust him at board, but tooke a house for him....

From *Brief Lives*, John Aubrey (1626-97).

63

Messalina

That Messalina, leaving the arms of her
twenty-five, or more, lovers—is, and I'm
translating literally: *still ardent,* the words
become a bit coarse in French, even
among men, and the Latin is self-explanatory.

Alfred Jarry, The Supermale. Trans.
Barbara Wright & Ralph Gladstone.

∾

Song for Silkworms

Every province and kingdom under heaven, no city has
avoided shield and sword. Why can't the weapons be
cast into ploughshares, and every inch of abandoned
field tilled by oxen? Don't condemn heroes to weep
like heavy rains, leave man to grain, women to silk....

Tu Fu (abridged). Trans. David Hinton.

∾

The Marvelous Ass

The tale spread far and wide. My exploits
soon made my master an illustrious personage.
"There goes the man," folks said, "who dines
with an ass, a dancing ass that understands
human speech and can answer with signs."

Apuleius, from The Golden Ass. Trans. Jack Lindsay.

The Grasp of Love

I thought there could be
No more love left anywhere.
Whence then is come this love,
That has caught me now
And holds me in its grasp?

Princess Hirokawa (8th century). Trans. Donald Keene.

∾

Die Verwirrung

All those eggheads going crazy trying to figure
out what makes things tick. Don't they know
that "Unser Philosophie ist eine Berichtigung des
Sprachgebrauch?" A smart fellow named Otto
Kretschmer told me that in a Vienna bierstube.

∾

De Perennitate

When Montesquiou was posing for his
portrait by Whistler, one day he got restless
and moved his eyes away from the artist,
who suggested: "If you will look at me for
an instant longer, you will look forever."

Man Pines to Live

Man pines to live but cannot endure the days
of his life. The learned covet the customs of
the savages. They envy the panther. The poet
wants to be an animal. "Submit, my heart. Sleep
the sleep of the brute," said Baudelaire.

Edward Dahlberg, from *The Sorrows of Priapus.*

∾

The Ceaseless Rain

It rains gently and unceasingly, it rains
listlessly but with infinite patience, as
it has always rained upon this earth, which
is the same color as the sky—somewhere between
soft green and soft ashengray....

Camilo José Cela, from *Mazurka for Two Dead Men.*
Trans. Patricia Hougaard.

∾

Nero Poisons Britannicus

He demanded a poison that should be most quick
and made a trial thereof in a kid and then in
a pig. When the pig died he commanded it be
given to Britannicus as he sat at supper with
him, who no sooner tasted it than he fell dead....

From *Lives of the Twelve Caesars,* Suetonius.
Trans. Philemon Holland.

De Senectute: Mary Baker Eddy

Mary Baker Eddy wrote that man
is neither old nor young. He is
a spiritual idea that never dies.
I no longer fear the first knock.
Let the door open wide, I'm ready.

∾

The Decline and Fall of the Roman Empire

When Edward Gibbon presented a volume
of his *Decline and Fall* to George III
(who was the crazy king) the monarch
said, "Another damn thick book, always
scribble, scribble, eh, Mr. Gibbon."

∾

Not My Loneliness, But Ours

The most of men are all too much myself,
my shed externals, as feces, hair, skin,
discarded clothes, useless to me and dead.
From oneness, what should we say we hadn't said
before together? Nothing to say to them....

William Bronk, from *The World, the Worldless* (1964). Abridged.

Not Waving But Drowning

Nobody heard him, the dead man,
But still he lay moaning:
I was much farther out than you thought
And not waving but drowning.
Poor chap, he always loved larking....

Stevie Smith, from Collected Poems. Abridged.

❧

Carriages

If the carriages of Kings and Princes bore
like moderation in peace, as they afford
in Tempests of Warre, surely the estates
of Kingdomes and the affayres of this world
would longer flourish and be better governed.

Sallust, The Conspiracy of Catiline. Trans. Thomas Heywood.

❧

A Difficult Courtship

Genji thought long about her. Though she had
with so strange and inexplicable a resolution
steeled her heart against him to the end,
each time he had remembered that she had gone
forever it filled him with depression.

Lady Murasaki, The Tale of Genji. Trans. Arthur Waley.

The Novelist, Maude Hutchins

M. H. had imagination, but when she was planning
a new novel she scribbled phrases and plot twists
on 3x5 cards which she'd store in a jade vase.
Ready to write, she'd dump the cards on the
floor, get down on her knees and arrange a book.

∽

On Her Prettiness

What the eye of the beholder sees
has *existenz*. Was it not Ignatius
of Freiburg who proved in 1166
that the waterfall only exists
because we can see it or hear it?

∽

Penelope to Ulysses

Penelope to the tardy Ulysses:
do not answer these lines, but come, for
Troy is dead and the daughters of Greece
rejoice. But all of Troy and Priam himself
are not worth the price I've paid for victory.

Ovid, Heroides. Trans. Howard Isbell.

The Coming of Spring

The Spring season is approaching,
Who will help me meeting with my dearest?
How shall I describe the beauty of the dearest,
Who is immersed in all beauties
That color all the pictures of the universe...?

> Kabir (1440-1518), abridged. Trans. Ezra Pound, adapted
> from an English version by Kali Mohan Ghose.

∾

Desire for the Impossible

Caligula: Now listen! I'm not mad; in fact I've
never felt so lucid. What happened to me is
quite simple; I suddenly felt a desire for
the impossible. That's all. Things as they
are, in my opinion, are far from satisfactory.

> Albert Camus, *Caligula*. Trans. unidentified.

∾

Odd Goings-on in Philadelphia

The painter Eakins was an odd duck. For him art
depended on the nude figure. But using nude
models wasn't enough. He wanted his girl students
to know the "joints and machinery" of the body.
He had himself photographed with them in the buff.

The Omniscient Autodidact

Kenneth Rexroth knew everything and would
tell you about it. He had a photographic
memory. After lunch he would lie in his
bathtub for two hours doing some light
reading, such as a history of Chinese science.

∾

Conscience at Yale

L's wealth made him feel guilty. Once a week
a poor boy came to his college room to help
him with his beetle collection. When rumors
spread of what L had given the maid at term's
end, the woman was fired by the house master.

∾

Dove Sta Memoria

In memory's locus taketh he his state
formed there in manner as a mist of light
upon a dusk that is come from Mars and stays.
Love is created, hath a sensate name,
his modus takes from soul, from heart his will.

Guido Cavalcanti (1255-1300). Trans. Ezra Pound.

The Pissing of the Toads

Concerning the venomous urine of toads, conceptions
are entertained which require consideration. That a
Toad pisseth, and this way diffuseth its venome,
is generally received, not only with us but also
in other parts, as the learned Scaliger observed.

Thomas Browne, *Pseudodoxia Epidemica,*
Enquiries into Certain Vulgar Errors (1646).

∿

Public Relations

Martial urged his friend Faustinus
to work faster on his book and to be
seen in the right company. What
you do *now* will count. Glory comes
late to the ashes of the great dead.

∿

In Love with You

In love with you
I have lost all sense of
Hiding from men's eyes.
If in exchange for meeting you
Is death so great a price to pay?

Ariwara no Narihiro (c. 860). Trans. Donald Keene.

The Old Man's Solution

He was losing his memory so he had
a surgeon insert his mind in her head
to remember things. She was good on
names and dates, but most remarkably
she'd recall things that never happened.

∾

The Birth of an Emperor

Claudius was born at Lyons, in the year when
Julius Antonius and Fabius Africanus were
consuls, upon the Kalends of August, that
very day on which an altar there was dedicated
to Augustus. Tiberius Claudius Drusus was his name.

Suetonius, *The Lives of the Twelve Caesars.*
Trans. Philemon Holland.

∾

The Abyss

Pascal's abyss went with him, yawned in the air.
—Alas! All is abyss! Desire, act, dream,
Word—I have felt the wind of terror stream
Many a time across my upright hair,
Above, below, around me, shores descending....

Baudelaire, *Flowers of Evil.*
Trans. Jackson Mathews.

The Other Shore of the Sea

It is time, love, to break off the somber rose,
shut up the stars and bury the ash in the earth;
and, in the rising of the light, wake with
those awaking, or go in the dream, reaching the
other shore of the sea which has no other shore.

> Pablo Neruda, from a tape. Trans. Alastair Reid.

❧

Premula's Problem

Quintius, her mentor, tries to make
love to her. She rather likes him
because his learning enlarges her head.
But he, poor old man, cannot enlarge
himself in bed. It's quite a problem.

> After Catullus.

❧

The Persian Woman

The fair one comes forth muffled and wrapped; the beast,
her dromedary, kneels; she mounts, turning her
latticed head toward us; I hear a tiny giggle; she
whispers to a slave girl nearby; the auditor also
laughs; they draw the little curtains; the camels start....

> Sir Richard Francis Burton, *Personal Narrative of a
> Pilgrimage to Al-Madinah and Meccah.* Ed. Edward Rice.

Providence, Fortune & Fate

Whilst a man confideth in Providence, he should not
slacken his exertions; for without labor he is
unable to obtain the oil from the seed. Fortune
attendeth that lion amongst men who exerteth himself.
They are meek who declare fate the sole cause.

From the Sanskrit, Vishnu-Sarma's *Hitopadela*
(*c.* 1002 A.D.).

∾

Remembrance of Her

No man can ever pass a day in boredom
   who has remembrance of her,
for she is the beginning and birth of all joy:
   and he who would praise her
no matter how well he speaks of her, he lies!

Peire Vidal (1175-1205) Trans. Paul Blackburn.

∾

The Ravaged Virgin

Aphrodisia in Anatolia is famed in mythic
history because it is recorded in Hesiod's
Theogony that there Zeus raped the nymph
Cleonia. He did it by disguising himself
as a water buffalo. She said it hurt a lot.   .

The Soldier Poet

Archilochos was the second great Greek poet,
next after Homer. His name means First Sergeant;
he was a mercenary. Satire and toasty lyrics
were his forte. Menander called him a "thistle
with graceful leaves." Wasps infest his tomb.

~

The Snake Game

Henry looked like a shoeclerk but was a spell-
binder. He persuaded a friend to let him put a
garter snake into her vulva. Exciting at first
but then the snake wouldn't be pulled out. He
had to take her to the hospital emergency room.

Henry Miller.

~

The Smart Man

That old know-it-all Cicero said that
the wicked flourish like a green bay
tree, and that an old love pinches like
a crab. A smart man but nobody liked him
much and Augustus had him executed.

Renaissance Politics

Since the Pope will soon die, the Bishop of Gurk
has been dispatched to Rome to help us behind the
papal throne. This matter will require a notable
sum of money. We hope that your bank will be able
to advance us a loan of up to three hundred ducats.

From "Hapsburgs and Fuggers" in *The Portable
Renaissance Reader*, eds. Ross & McLaughlin.

∾

Salad Dressing and an Artichoke

It was please it was please carriage cup in an ice-
cream, in an ice cream it was too bended bended with
scissors and all this time. A whole is inside a part, a
part does go away, a whole is red leaf. No choice was
where there was and a second and a second.

Gertrude Stein, from *Tender Buttons* (1914).

∾

The Sweet Singer

Sappho led a band of lovely girls
on Lesbos, and she sang to them
sweet singing: "Desire has shaken
my mind as wind in the mountain
forest roars through the trees."

The Shadowy Figure

Behind the moving screen of years there
is, unseen by passers-by, a shadowy
figure. Even among his friends few know
that he exists. But the figure knows who
he is and is reconciled to being a shadow.

∾

The Smile of the Desert

In the desert I felt a thrill of pleasure—such as only
the captive delivered from his dungeon can experience.
The sunbeams warmed me into renewed life and vigour,
the air of the Desert was a perfume, and the homely face
of Nature was as a smile of a dear old Friend.

> Sir Richard Burton, *Personal Narrative of a
> Pilgrimage to Al-Madinah and Meccah.*

∾

The Sculptor

Brancusi didn't have much to say but he
cooked a great Romanian stew and liked
after eating to swing upside down by his
knees on a monkey's trapeze while his
phonograph blared out Ravel's *Bolero*.

On Spells

"Begging priests and soothsayers will go to
the wealthy and convince them that if you want
to harm an enemy, at very little expense,
they will persuade the gods through charms
and binding spells to do your bidding."

Plato, trans. W.B. Fleischman

∾

Artaud on Van Gogh

He is a painter because he recollected nature as if he
had re-perspired it and made it sweat, made it spurt
forth in luminous beams onto his canvas, in monumental
clusters of colors ... the fearful pressure of apostrophes,
stripes, commas, bars ... ocular clashes taken from life....

Antonin Artaud, abridged. Trans. Mary Beach.

∾

To Surya

His bright rays bear him up aloft, the god who
knoweth all that lives. The constellations pass
away, like thieves, together with their beams,
before the all-beholding sun. Swift and beautiful
art thou, O Surya, maker of the light.

A hymn from the Rig-Veda (1200 B.C. or earlier).
Ed. from Sanskrit by Nicol Macnicol. Abridged.

Sir Walter Raleigh:
A Double Pentastich

Raleigh loved a wench well; and one time getting
up one of the Mayds of Honour against a tree in a
Wood who seemed at first boarding to be something
fearful of her Honour, she cryed, "Sweet Sir
Walter, will you undoe me?" At last as the danger

and the pleasure at the same time grew higher,
she cried in extasey, "Sisser Swatter Sisser
Swatter." She proved with child, and I doubt not
but this Hero took care of them both, as also
that the Product was more than an ordinary mortal.

❧

A Statement for El Greco and
William Carlos Williams

Toledo shines out like no other city.
And Poe has risen
With his variable ways, and his jaw set
    at an angle.
Toledo, with no name carved to it saying:
    here lies...
Toledo, with the face of no man
    at the window.

Kay Boyle, from A Glad Day (1938).

Slaves of the Gods

Lucian of Samosata was not taken in by
the gods. "Why do men make sacrifices
to the gods? They are fellow slaves with
men. With the gods the thing goes on to
infinity. And your slavery will be eternal."

See Lucian's *Zeus Catechised.*

∾

Those Wonderful People

Well all right if that's the
way it is that's how it is and
I'll just have to put you
back in my special box that's
labeled "wonderful people."

∾

Touching

I'd like to touch you in beautiful
places, places that no one else
has ever found, places we found
together when we were in Otherwhere,
such beautiful hidden places.

The Tender Letter

C'était à Paris. She was Jeanine, young, pretty and
bright. Une jeune fille bien élevée. They often had
me to Sunday dinner. I thought we were just friends.
Then the note to my hotel: "Je voudrais être ta
maîtresse." In three months she was dead of cancer.

～

A Solution

If a poet can't get the girl
he wants with his words he'd
better get out of the poetry
business and go to work on Wall
Street and try to buy her.

～

Sugaring Time

It's sugaring time and the buckets are hanging
from the maples. I can hear the plip-plip of
the drops falling into them. An old man
rounds the bend. He's staggering drunk from
the water he's been stealing from the buckets.

The Rescue

From New Orleans Tenn wrote me a wonderfully
comical letter. He was being relentlessly
pursued by a pretty girl. She was cramping
his style; would I get her off his back? A
very sexy girl; she soon had me on *my* back.

❧

Spring Comes Again

The spaces in time seem to be narrowing.
Days rush along as if they were running a
race. But the marching order of daffodils,
hyacinths, and white clouds of shad blow
are as military as when I was a child.

❧

The Magic Flute

That summer in Munich we were Papageno and Papagena.
We walked along the Isar and in the Englische Garten
and went to a different opera almost every night. But
it was Mozart who set us dreaming and made us fall
in love. Beautiful days and now happy memories.

A Moment of Vanity

A moment of happy vanity came to me in Urbino,
the seat of the one-eyed condottiero, Duke "Feddy,"
who gathered so many artists and scholars at his
court. I was dickering for a book and the seller
told me, "Lei se defende bene in Italiano."

> "You defend yourself well in Italian."

~

In Memory of Robert Fitzgerald

O best of friends it's years since you crossed
the Lethe but still you often visit me in happy
memories: how you cocked your head when you were
talking, how you helped me with my Greek, and
our battles as Achilles and Hektor on the links.

~

Your Love

Your love reminds me of the
sense of humor of one of those
funny plumbers who like to switch
the handles on the hot and cold
faucets in hotel wash basins.

The Life of Words

When he was young he read many books,
he devoured them. Later he tried to be a
writer. But he discovered that words
have a life of their own, often not
saying what he wanted them to say.

∾

Living in Three Worlds

I live in three worlds, the one around
me and the one in my thoughts where you
live and the one in my old books where
I can read what you and I did when we
were once together in another life.

∾

An Admonition

To tie a girl up with string as if she
were a package for future delivery is
no longer an acceptable procedure.
Times have changed and certain atti-
tudes must now be reconsidered.

Ars Gratia Artis

In the next chair of the barber shop the
director of the world's greatest museum
with its $28 million Rembrandt was catching
hell from the barber for having ruined the
line of his sideburns with an electric razor.

∾

The Healer

Ben Wiesel, my beloved shrink, who rescued me from
the Slough of Despond, knew the right way to treat
a mad poet. Each session he would ask to see
my new poems. He commented on them with care
and I never had to utter a single word.

∾

The First Night

we spent together was like
school. Each was trying to
teach the other what we
liked or did not like. Love
was becoming a real thing.

Elusive Time

In love it may be dangerous to reckon on
time or count on it. Time's here and then
it's gone. I'm not thinking of death but
of the slippage, the unpredictable loss of
days on which we counted for happiness.

❧

The Evening Star

You came as a thought when I was
past such thinking. You came as a
song when I was finished singing.
You came when the sun had begun
its setting. You were my evening star.

❧

The Discovery

When will he discover that he's a joke, that the
smiles that greet him in the post office are really
hidden laughter, suppressed by politeness, that
when he leaves they laugh about him and his
pretensions to being an important poet and big brain.

The Dance of the Skin

Over your flesh the skin dances.
But don't try to talk about the
dancing of the skin. Better to
say nothing at all. Just lie still
and feel it move. Just lie still.

∾

The Bird of Endless Time

Your fingers touch me like a bird's wing,
like the feathers of the bird that returns
every hundred years to brush against a peak
in the Himalayas until the rock's been
worn away and the kalpas are ended.

Kalpa: in Hinduism an eon.

∾

Ars Poetica

Some think poetry should be
adorned or complicated. But I'll
take the simple statement in
plain speech. I think that
will do all that I want to do.

All Good Things Pass

The girl at the order desk of the University
Press from whom I used to buy my Loeb Library
classics is now a telephone hitched to a
computer. She would wrap her long legs around
my neck and I imagined she was Tara of Cos.

∾

An Apology

She said, in apology, they aren't
very big, are they? But I told her:
let us not be concerned with the
minute particulars, it is only
your inner light that I cherish.

∾

I Don't Know Where She Is Wandering Tonight

Someone saw her in Ectaban and another in
Samarkand. The world is full of seductions
for a beautiful girl. I'll send word by
carrier pigeon that there will always be
lodging for her in my ever faithful heart.

A Proposal

I want to breathe you in, not the
sweet odor of your skin but your
breath. As close as that, the two
of us breathing as one, one body,
one person, and one soul.

∿

The Stargazer

A lovely girl, but after we'd had a few dates she
let me know, quite kindly, that I wasn't intelligent
enough to attract her. How right she was! Today she
is eminent in the field of astro-ethnography. She
plots the movement by the stars of primitive peoples.

∿

The Scar

You have burned yourself deep
into me. I know now that you
don't love me enough but the
burn scar is inside me and
I think it will never heal.

The Tribute

You know how a cat will bring a
mouse it has caught and lay it at
your feet. So I bring you new
poems as my tribute to your
beauty and promise of my love.

The Toast

Past midnight. I'm in bed
sipping the glass of juice
and vodka that helps me sleep.
Each sip is a toast to one of
the girls I loved in the past.

The Wisdom of the Owl

Your error said the owl was dehumani-
zation. It wasn't a girl you wanted
but a love object, and for what you
were willing to give you couldn't
expect one that would turn you alive.

*This is the last book of his own that James Laughlin helped
to prepare during his lifetime. The manuscript had been
completed and sent to the typesetter before the onset of his
final illness and death in November 1997. He saw and
approved everything in it except this colophon.*